■ SCHOLASTIC

News

Nonfiction Readers

From Pit to Peach Tree

by Ellen Weiss

Children's Press®
A Division of Scholastic Inc.
New York Toronto London Auckland Sydney
Mexico City New Delhi Hong Kong
Danbury, Connecticut

These content vocabulary word builders are for grades 1–2.

Subject Consultant: Emily Yates, Millennium Seed Bank Project Co-coordinator, Institute for Plant Biology and Conservation, Chicago Botanic Garden, Glencoe, Illinois

Reading Consultant: Cecilia Minden-Cupp, PhD, Early Literacy Consultant and Author, Chapel Hill, North Carolina

Book Design: Simonsays Design!
Book Production: The Design Lab

Library of Congress Cataloging-in-Publication Data
Weiss, Ellen, 1949–
From pit to peachtree / by Ellen Weiss.
    p. cm.—(Scholastic news nonfiction readers)
Includes bibliographical references.
  ISBN-13: 978-0-531-18538-4 (lib. bdg.) 978-0-531-18791-3 (pbk.)
  ISBN-10: 0-531-18538-9 (lib. bdg.) 0-531-18791-8 (pbk.)
1. Peach—Juvenile literature. 2. Peach—Life cycles—Juvenile literature. I. Title. II. Series.
QK495.R78W64 2008
634'.25—dc22   3539   2007010068

CONTENTS

WORD HUNT

Look for these words as you read. They will be in **bold**.

blossoms
(**blah**-suhmz)

pollen
(**pol**-uhn)

roots
(roots)

orchards
(**or**-churdz)

pit
(pit)

seed
(seed)

stem
(stem)

5

It's the Pits!

This tree is full of yummy, ripe peaches.

Peaches have a hard stone, or **pit**, in the center.

Pits hold something important inside their hard shells.

pit

There is a pit inside
each of these peaches.

A pit has a **seed** inside.

The seed can grow into a new peach tree.

The pit has to crack open before the seed can start to grow.

seed

This pit was split open
to show the seed inside.

Sometimes animals can help a pit crack open.

Squirrels and other animals like to eat peaches.

The peach pit may crack open if an animal chews on it.

A ground squirrel eats a peach.

Most peaches are grown on farms called **orchards**.

Peach farmers use machines to crack open the pits. Then they plant the seeds.

A seed sends **roots** down into the soil. A **stem** and leaves appear above the soil.

orchard

roots

stem ➡

Over time, the stem grows taller.

It hardens into a tree trunk.

In a few years, the peach tree will grow flowers.

Then the tree is ready to grow peaches!

Farmers plant peach trees in rows.

In the spring, a peach tree is covered with pink **blossoms**.

The blossoms contain tiny grains called **pollen**.

Wind and insects carry the pollen from one blossom to another. Then peaches can begin to grow.

pollen

These peach trees are full of blossoms.

Over the summer, the peaches will grow big and ripen.

People will pick peaches for eating.

Other ripe peaches will fall off the tree to the ground.

When peaches fall, new peach trees might grow!

PEACH TREE LIFE CYCLE

1 The peach pit cracks open. The seed falls to the ground.

2 A small plant grows from the seed.

5

Peaches grow and ripen. Some fall to the ground.

4

The tree blossoms.

3

A young peach tree forms.

YOUR NEW WORDS

blossoms (**blah**-suhmz) flowers on fruit trees or other plants

orchards (**or**-churdz) farms where fruit trees are grown

pit (pit) the hard stone that holds a seed inside some kinds of fruits

pollen (**pol**-uhn) tiny, yellow grains made by plants, which are needed for new plants to grow

roots (roots) the parts of plants that grow underground and absorb water from the soil

seed (seed) the part of a flowering plant from which a new plant can grow

stem (stem) the main part of a plant from which leaves and flowers grow

OTHER FRUITS WITH PITS

apricots
(**a**-pri-kots)

cherries
(**cher**-eez)

nectarines
(nek-tuh-**reenz**)

plums
(plumz)

INDEX

FIND OUT MORE

Book:

Hughes, Meredith Sayles. *Tall and Tasty: Fruit Trees.* Minneapolis: Lerner Publications, 2000.

Website:

SpringboardMagazine.com—The Circle of Life
http://www.springboardmagazine.com/science/lifecircle.htm

MEET THE AUTHOR

Ellen Weiss has received many awards for her books for kids. She has a garden, where she is especially good at growing weeds.